Dedicated to my Life Mapping guinea pigs
who believed coaching was part of my purpose:
Keisha, Sandy, Megs, Aaron, and Heidi.
Thank you.

Why Life Mapping?

How are you approaching your life? Haphazardly or intentionally?

I confess, although I knew what I wanted to do when I grew-up, I pursued it in the most all-over-the-place and unsustainable way. And even then, I was so focused on what I wanted to do, I didn't consider who I wanted to be.

Too frequently, the best-laid plans don't empower us to become who we are really designed to be or help us make the difference we were born to make. They send us in the wrong direction. And even then, we don't usually have a system for functionally thriving within our chosen path. Although this way of living is the norm for most adults, I'm here to tell you that there is more for you. You have a story to live, and here is a method for you to make that happen.

For many years I struggled with overwhelm, and I was showing symptoms of burnout. My desire to "change the world" and my involvement in advocacy work were beginning to hurt my relationships with those who were most important to me: God, my family, and my community. It took years of relearning and recognizing my limits to change that. In retrospect, I see how the way I pursued purpose was directly related to my misunderstanding of who I am meant to be (my identity) and not having a realistic action-plan that aligned with my beliefs.

> "If you don't prioritize your life someone else will."
> —Greg McKeown

Your Life Approach

My clients tend to fall into one of two camps: Big Purpose or Little Purpose.

I am an example of Big Purpose, which isn't uncommon among us changemakers. But I see Little Purpose just as frequently. <u>Circle the phrases you relate to the most in both categories:</u>

Big Purpose:

Do you ever feel like you'd like to do all the things, but you aren't sure where to start? Or, on the other hand, maybe you feel unfulfilled and burnt-out, already doing too much. You might have a vision you don't know how to get to. Your dreams are so big, you're unsure if they're even worth reaching for—but you might try anyway!

Little Purpose:

Then there is the other end of the spectrum—no dreams or vision in sight. You might feel content with where you are, but are wondering if your life actually should have a purpose or meaning. You're afraid you'll have no legacy. Cynicism might have you in a head-lock, believing there is no point in trying to create social change. You might feel skepticism about any mystical sounding comments like, "I was born for this." However, these attitudes aren't serving you anymore.
Your life is going nowhere quickly.

It doesn't matter which camp you fall in. What matters is that you want to begin living intentionally. This is good. This is where we all start.

LIFE MAPPING, PAGE 2

An Intentional Life

Only after I took the time to stop, recuperate, and rest, could I reconsider how to move forward. I wanted to do things differently, but I wasn't sure how until I encountered a life coaching technique called life planning. First, I made my destination who I wanted to be—identity first rather that what I thought I wanted to do. I began to learn about my personality, values, gifts, and skills. I named all the areas that refilled me and gave me purpose so that I could prioritize them. I began implementing goals and time-boundaries to take action that aligned with these priorities. I stopped letting life control me and began Life Mapping.

I imagined my personal Life Map, an ever-changing plan, like a pin-point on a map. Not only did it give me a destination to head towards, but it anchored me to a path, realigning me to what mattered. I stopped feeling overwhelmed all the time. I was able to accept my limits. I found joy connecting with God, my family, and my community. I figured out how to meet my own needs and care for myself. I became intentional about how I gave back to the world, both through my career and in my free time.

Life Mapping helps us move at the right pace, go the right away, and live out our purpose.

Not surprisingly, it turns out I wasn't alone in my struggle to live intentionally. The mission of my coaching business, Average Advocate, is to empower everyday people to be changemakers with more confidence and less overwhelm. I realized I couldn't just direct my readers to get engaged in social issues, speak a motivational message, or consult for their social good orgs and projects. To truly empower my people, and hopefully help them avoid my mistakes, I actually needed to share this framework I've used since 2016. Now coaching others is one of my greatest joys.

About Life Mapping

To be clear, Life Mapping is not something I invented on my own. I first learned about life planning from Michael Hyatt and Daniel Harkavy. Since then, I've discovered bookshelves of life coaching guidance and was trained in co-active coaching in a cohort (specifically for writers) by Kate Riney.

Life Mapping is simply one of the versions of life coaching I use, a compilation of exercises with tweaks that I've seen work best with those I've led. In addition, I added a QR code at the end of this workbook for resources and online tools that might be useful as you practice Life Mapping. Although Life Mapping is a great way to discover purpose and make a plan as a one-time thing, it is most effective if implemented overtime as a "living" map. Ideally, you'd make new goals every three months. Alternatively, you can pull it out to revamp and realign your direction after an extended time away from it. Personally, I use the online template to make this easier.

Starting and then sticking with your Life Map requires time commitment and often accountability. I recommend finding a partner who you can process with and get feedback from as you tackle this together. I also offer one-on-one and group coaching to guide you. Head over to my website, www.AverageAdvocate.com to schedule a free no-pressure discovery call.

Whether you create your Life Map on your own, with a friend, or with me, I can't wait to hear how it goes! I have confidence this will help you become who you're meant to be, which will in turn bring what good only you can bring into the world! I am excited for you to take this step forward to discover your purpose and make a plan to live intentionally.

Elisa Johnston
YOUR LIFE MAPPING GUIDE

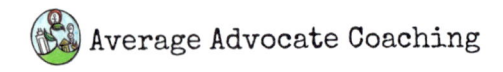

Average Advocate Coaching

WWW.AVERAGEADVOCATE.COM

Be/Do

Now that you've read some of my story as an example, but before you begin Life Mapping yourself, let's clarify what Life Mapping helps us accomplish. We need to recognize that the direction we move towards is always driven by two parts. To simplify, I call this our *Be* and our *Do*.

BE = DESTINATION

Your identity is what makes you tick. It is how you define and who you let yourself be defined by. It is your personality, talents, gifts, and passions all wrapped into one. Overtime, our identities can pivot to a degree. As we become more healthy and holistic individuals, we move towards our best selves. What fulfills us isn't just for our own happiness, either. Research continually shows us that we find meaning when we give back to the world. Each of us are fulfilled by giving ourselves to others in a unique way. Becoming who we are meant to be is a process that never ends. It is the direction we want to point our compass to. This growing awareness of your identity and the purpose you are drawn to is your *Be*.

DO = PATH

Pointing towards your *Be*, you can design a flexible path for intentional and impactful living. All your actions, accomplishments, pursuits, ways you serve, give, roles you play, and how you spend your time becomes your *Do*. It is important to recognize that your *Do* isn't totally in your control. It is often affected by your abilities, access to resources, and relationships. In addition, it changes through the seasons. There are many expressions of your *Do* that can reflect who you are meant to *Be*.

BE (DESTINATION) + DO (PATH) = YOUR INTENTIONAL & IMPACTFUL LIFE!

It is essential to keep your *Be* as your destination, informing your *Do* (path to get there). When these are reversed, we stop living intentionally and usually end up unsatisfied. Keep *Be* as your North Star, and you'll always be able to live a story worth living. The steps on the following pages are designed to help you to clarify both your *Be* and your *Do*. We'll come back to these summary terms at the end of the Life Mapping process!

WWW.AVERAGEADVOCATE.COM

Life Mapping Steps

1.) BEGIN AT THE END

2.) LIFE THEMES

3.) PRIORITY ACCOUNTS

4.) PURPOSE STATEMENTS

5.) IDEAL FUTURE

6.) CURRENT REALITY

7.) 90-DAY GOALS

8.) INSPIRATIONAL QUOTES

9.) SCHEDULE BLOCKING

10.) IMPLEMENTATION SYSTEM

Crafting Your Life Map

Ready to begin? A Life Map is a forever draft: it is a changing, living document that you continue charting. Although some might do it in one day, most of my clients schedule six sessions to work through it. Remember, it is only the initial design that takes a significant amount of time. After that, you only need to dedicate time for charting when you're ready to make new goals. Lastly, each time you start working on steps 2-5, glance at the "Begin at the End" section to refocus on who you want to be.

Setting Yourself Up For Success
Check the boxes as you complete each tip:

- ☐ Choose a block of time (even if just one full morning) for its initial conception
- ☐ Plan for a babysitter if you need one (or do a kid exchange with a friend for affordability)
- ☐ Choose a space where you won't be easily distracted and can start with a clear-head
- ☐ Don't beat yourself up for having a hard time focusing and getting into it
- ☐ Schedule in advance when you will work on the other steps
- ☐ Do something meaningful to mark this, to begin memorably. Go on a retreat, get a special drink, and/or give yourself something small as memorabilia
- ☐ Remind yourself again that this *cannot* be perfect—don't try to make it perfect!
- ☐ If you prefer drafting it on a computer, go to the QR code in the back of this workbook to grab the free template I use

Here's an example: I started my Life Map on a morning when my husband committed to care for the kids. I went on a walk to pray and clear my head. I found a flower to press as memorabilia. Then I settled in at a library for hours. Lastly, I ate lunch at a cafe where I kept at it. I continued working on it at home for a few more weeks.

WWW.AVERAGEADVOCATE.COM
STEP 1

Begin At The End

Imagine you're nearing or at the end of your life. Choose the perspective that helps you the most:

1.) You're watching your funeral unseen, listening to the eulogy. Everyone you know is there to celebrate your life and mourn your passing.

2.) You have reached your 101st birthday. Every loved one came to throw a party in your honor!

For this exercise to be successful, you must try to really feel the gravity of who you want to be at the end of your life.

Write this in first person, as if you embody the person speaking about you. For example, "Charlie was the most generous person. I respected him because he often…" Use as much space as needed to really get it out, using extra paper or writing it in an online document if preferred. Write out at least four different speeches about your life to get other perspectives. The following pages will give you the most common relationships to start with. Be aware that Begin at the End usually takes an hour. It is often uncomfortable and you might cry. However, this exercise typically reveals the seed of who you desire to be, what is planted deep within you.

In these margins, name some people you'd like to be there. Then name some people who you'd prefer not to be there.

WWW.AVERAGEADVOCATE.COM
STEP 1

Begin At The End

What would you want God to say about you?
(Or alternatively, a hero or a mentor?)

What would you want your spouse (or significant other) to say about you?

PAGE 8

WWW.AVERAGEADVOCATE.COM
STEP 1

Begin At The End

What would you want your children to say about you?

What would you want your friends and community to say about you?

What would you want your co-workers to say about you?

PAGE 9

Life Themes

WWW.AVERAGEADVOCATE.COM
STEP 2

Life Themes act like GPS destinations points. They give us purpose. Together, they become our "why" and our North Star.

This is my favorite part to do in Life Mapping! It is time to analyze your Begin at the End and search for common themes. Look for statements that are similar. Each category becomes a Life Theme. Write them in the circles below as you begin to notice them. Most people have 5-12 Life Themes.

For example, I discovered a major theme in my Begin at the End when I noticed these phrases all throughout my eulogy: "Elisa brings life," "She helps people feel alive and joyful," "She gives life," "Elisa made a life-giving home for us," and "Elisa lived fully alive." These are all similar, a Life Theme. My desire to help others feel and experience an intentional thriving life is one of the ways I am uniquely designed. (It is also why I became a coach!)

Remember, there are no right or wrong answers. As you begin to look for themes in your life they'll become more obvious. And some themes you aren't sure of are actually themes that will fade away or combine under a new name. Occasionally, clients are disappointed by this exercise, realizing their Life Themes aren't something magical, but are already a foundation to who they are. Regardless of how you feel in response to this exercise, once they are named, you become more intentional about them.

I believe these Life Themes help you determine who you desire to be and how you're best suited to give back to the world.

"If you don't know where you're going, any road will take you there."
—George Harrison

PAGE 10

Life Themes

WWW.AVERAGEADVOCATE.COM
STEP 2

Here are some methods to do this exercise:

- Highlight/circle similar phrases in your Begin at the End
- Sort potential themes into categories with Post-It-Notes or on a blank paper as you read your Begin at the End out loud.
- Ask a friend who knows you well to read your Begin at the End and have them help you brainstorm with you.
- Then fill in these circles with common phrases. Each person usually has 5-12 major themes.

Here are some examples of Life Themes:

Loving well, bringing beauty, extending family to others, being inviting, generosity, developing community, pioneering ideas, being creative, mentoring, seeking justice, sharing stories, helping others be healthy, modeling loyalty and faithfulness, organization, closing gaps, productivity, listening and empathizing, solving problems, motivating others, providing, giving vision, teaching well, speaking truth, practicing welcome, developing efficiency, strengthening old things, creating process, serving in the background, hospitality, etc...

Here are some suggestions if you feel stuck:

- Add more details to your Begin at the End. Being more authentic, descriptive, and vulnerable allows for your Life Themes to peek through better.
- Life Themes and your personal values typically overlap. Do a values exercise to give yourself insight! (You can find one using the QR code in the back of the book on the free resource page.)
- Invite someone else into this exercise to provide a different perspective. You can also schedule a coaching session with me. I love helping my clients determine their Life Themes!

Life Themes

WWW.AVERAGEADVOCATE.COM
STEP 2

PAGE 12

Priority Accounts

WWW.AVERAGEADVOCATE.COM
STEP 3

In Step Three you will choose 6-12 Priority Accounts. On this page and the next, brainstorm by writing out everything important to you. These important things include relationships, what is necessary for you to survive and function, and some of the Life Themes from the last exercise. Then lump these into categories that you can use to create headers. These are your Priority Accounts.

Think of Priority Accounts as your most vital investments at a bank account. You never want them to drop into the red.

Pouring into these areas will give you an intentional, purposeful, and thriving life.

To the right, order your Priority Accounts by level of importance to you. (It is okay if they aren't perfectly in order.) Over time, you might realize you can combine some of these. Choose a name that inspires you rather than drains you. For example, "Life-Giving Home" is what I call my Priority Account for budgeting, meal-planning, cleaning, and other essential aspects of household management. This helps me purposefully engage in something that is a priority for me, but I don't enjoy.

PAGE 13

Priority Accounts
-BRAINSTORMING SPACE-

WWW.AVERAGEADVOCATE.COM
STEP 3

1.
2.
3.
4.
5.
6.
7.
8.
9.
10.

Here are some common categories:

God, faith, spouse, significant other, money, children (each child can have a separate category as well), career, extended family, education, hobbies, friends, community, self-care, health, volunteering, charity, self-development, pets, education, recreational activities, creativity, or areas of leadership or influence (but, remember roles change!)

PAGE 14

WWW.AVERAGEADVOCATE.COM
STEP 4

Purpose Statements

If someone (like God or the Universe) gave you a full bank account, wouldn't they tell you why? The currency of this bank account includes all available resources: time, money, energy, rapport, reputation, etc... Your account can be rich, full, depleted, or in debt. Using this context, write a purpose statement for each of your Priority Accounts below:

#1. _____
Purpose:

#2. _____
Purpose:

#3. _____
Purpose:

#4. _____
Purpose:

#5. _____
Purpose:

#6. _____
Purpose:

#7. _____
Purpose:

#8. _____
Purpose:

#9. _____
Purpose:

#10. _____
Purpose:

WWW.AVERAGEADVOCATE.COM
STEP 5 & 6

Ideal Future

In the section below write out what your ideal future would look like played out for each Priority Account. This step is all dreaming. What would the best version of your future look like for each priority area?

- Write this in present tense to make this more effective.
- This can be long and detailed, or short, but still having a concrete vision.

Here is an example of an Ideal Future for a "Health and Body" Priority Account:

"I maintain my daily hygiene. I am not addicted to substances and eat healthy 80% of the time. I take my vitamins. I walk 6000+ steps a day, exercise 4x a week, and strengthen my core muscles with yoga to reduce back pain. My body is fit enough to climb mountains. I sleep eight hours a night. I keep up with recommended check-ups. I take a weekly Sabbath. I rest my body an hour before bed."

As you can't change people, focus on where you have influence rather than changing the other person. Here are examples:

- "I am able to emotionally regulate during hard conversations with my spouse."
- "I am able to believe the truth of who I am, despite what my mom says about me."
- "I keep my boundaries when my family tries to manipulates me."

Current Reality

In the section below, make bullet-point lists depicting your current reality in comparison to your envisioned Ideal Future. Be sure to be honest, including the areas you are doing great in, alright in, bad in, and are totally a mess within. This is a self-evaluation.

Comparing where you want to be with where you are now becomes your catalyst and guide to make goals that give you forward momentum in the right direction. Through this process you should also be able to pinpoint what areas to pour more energy into without slowing down, halting to a stop, or becoming indebted in other priority areas. Write at least three positives and three areas you might be struggling in.

Here is an example of a Current Reality for a "Healthy Marriage" Priority Account:

- We spend significant time together doing puzzles
- We laugh together often
- We parent very differently, which becomes problematic
- I'm usually too tired to have sex
- I don't talk about my faith—maybe this makes me feel disconnected?
- We volunteer together monthly, which I really love

"SOMETIMES WHAT YOU DON'T DO IS JUST AS IMPORTANT AS WHAT YOU DO."
—Greg McKeown

Ideal Future & Current Reality

WWW.AVERAGEADVOCATE.COM
STEP 5 & 6

#1 IDEAL FUTURE

#1 CURRENT REALITY

#2 IDEAL FUTURE

#2 CURRENT REALITY

Ideal Future & Current Reality

WWW.AVERAGEADVOCATE.COM
STEPS 5 & 6

#3 IDEAL FUTURE

#3 CURRENT REALITY

#4 IDEAL FUTURE

#4 CURRENT REALITY

PAGE 18

Ideal Future & Current Reality

WWW.AVERAGEADVOCATE.COM
STEP 5 & 6

#5 IDEAL FUTURE

#5 CURRENT REALITY

#6 IDEAL FUTURE

#6 CURRENT REALITY

Ideal Future & Current Reality

WWW.AVERAGEADVOCATE.COM
STEP 5 & 6

#7 IDEAL FUTURE

#7 CURRENT REALITY

#8 IDEAL FUTURE

#8 CURRENT REALITY

PAGE 20

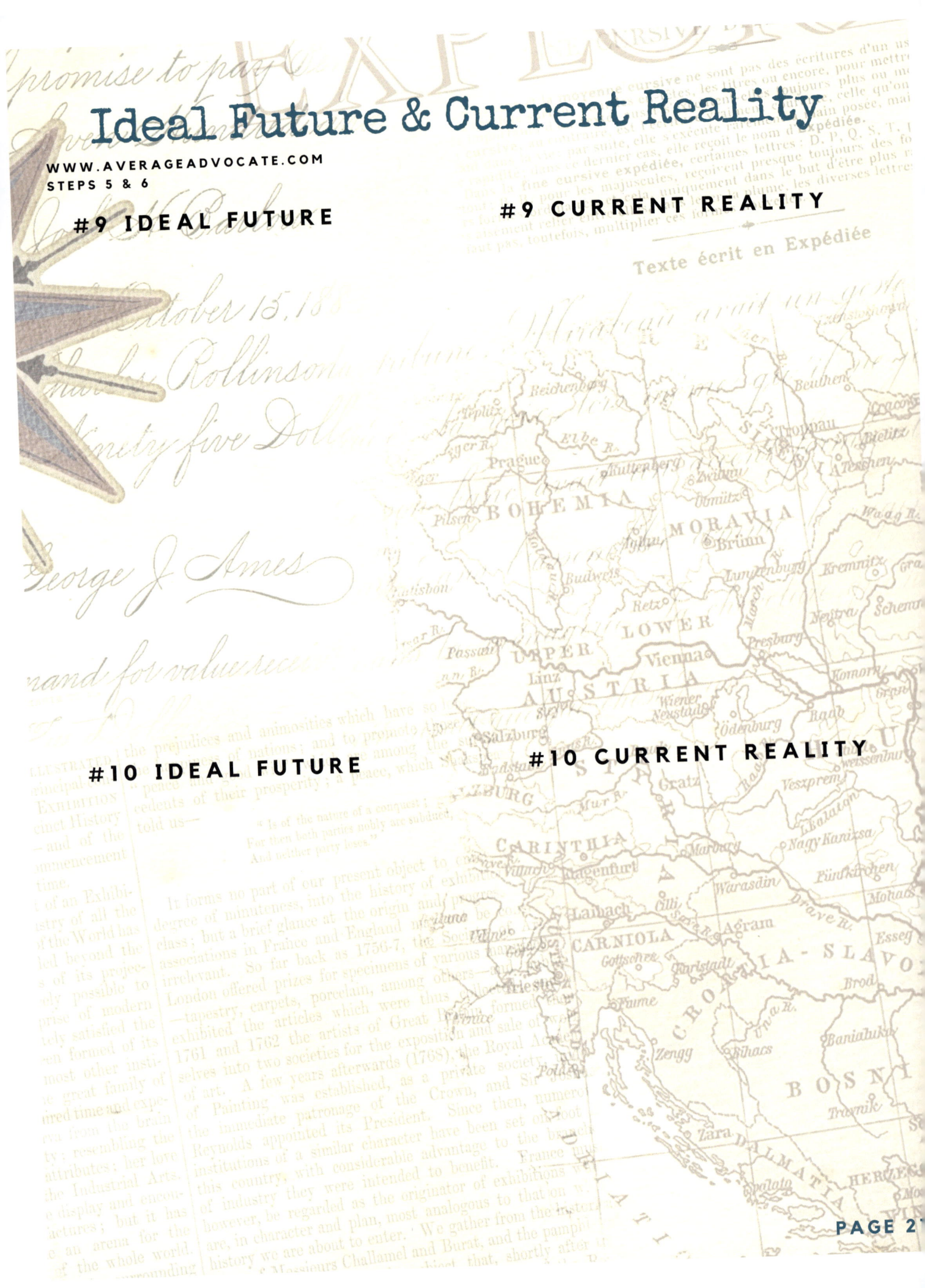

Ideal Future & Current Reality

WWW.AVERAGEADVOCATE.COM
STEPS 5 & 6

#9 IDEAL FUTURE

#9 CURRENT REALITY

#10 IDEAL FUTURE

#10 CURRENT REALITY

PAGE 21

WWW.AVERAGEADVOCATE.COM
STEP 7

90-Day Goals

In this section you will choose three reasonable goals for each of your priority accounts. This is how you make your vision become a reality: small steps over the course of each season. Even if it seems like you're not moving forward as quickly as you'd like, keep in mind that you're playing the long-game here!

It is okay to have more goals in some areas than others—just not so many that you won't have the time or energy to complete them. There are seasons when a few of your priority accounts must get almost all of your attention. But there is always something you can give to each area. It is important to make goals, even the smallest ones. Otherwise, you'll feel you've lost your vision.

To do this, you will have to choose reasonable goals. Later in your Life Map, you will do the Blocking Schedule exercise to help you see how much time you actually have available. This will likely cause you to go back and change some of your goals (and that is good).

Secondly, you will need these goals to be actionable. If you have to make ten decisions before you even embark on your project, the project isn't an actionable goal—but your decisions are.

Also, the more specific you are, the more likely you will be able to complete your goals.

The best goals are "SMART," or Specific, Measurable, Attainable, Relevant, and Time-bound. It also helps to word your goals in a positive way, instead of choosing a bunch of "do not's" and "no's." You might even want to find accountability or create specific rewards for goals that you need extra motivation to complete!

Lastly, sometimes goals won't work out. Expect this. These then become opportunities to reevaluate. Do you still want the outcome of that goal? Is this the right life-season for it? What can you do differently? You can try pairing what you don't like to do with something you do like. Consider incentives. Make it more manageable. Ask for help. Tweak your goal. Just don't get discouraged and quit.

On the following page I'm going to compare and contrast examples of different goals to help prepare you to make your own. Ready for it?

WWW.AVERAGEADVOCATE.COM
STEP 7

90-Day Goals

To help you out, I'm going to give you some examples of SMART goals that you can replicate.

Poor goals:

Bring in the big bucks!

Be healthy!

Find a new career

Invest in kids

Start painting again!

Try to convince my spouse to change responsibilities with me

Figure out spiritual life

Teach kids to not be jerks

Reconnect with my spouse

Ideal goals:

1.) Make a business plan by going through that workbook
2.) apply for a business license

1.) Talk with my spouse about options and accountability
2.) Schedule Dr. appointment 3.) Check if there is room in our budget for an eating plan, gym membership, or health coach
4.) Schedule two time blocks on my calendar to make a practical plan that I'll start in the next set of 90 Day Goals

1.) Take a Myers-Briggs personality test to see what careers are suggested for me 2.) Ask the boss if I can switch my hours for when I have more energy in the day 3.) Make a "Circle of influence" list of things I can do something about now to prep for my next 90-day goals

Ask each child what they'd want to do on a one-on-one date with me and do it over the next 90-days.

Tell the family it is art night every Tuesday after dinner. I'll paint and kids can join if they want.

1.) Every Monday night try to have a "household meeting" and suggest changes 2.) Text my support friend to update them on how it went or didn't go 3.) Download "Fair Play" cards and ask my spouse if they'll use them to do a renegotiation of responsibilities with me. (Be honest about feeling overloaded!)

1.) Join that small group 2.) Set a timer and write to God for five minutes 3.) Do a meditation prayer five nights a week before bed

Get a copy of Elisa's Justice-Minded Kids to do each Thursday night. (Here's my shameless pitch!)

1.) Ask neighbors to kid swap on Saturdays so we can go out twice a month. 2.) Go to bed at the same time every-other-day
3.) Give spouse a massage once a week (Wednesday night?)

WWW.AVERAGEADVOCATE.COM
STEP 7

90-Day Goals

#1 ——————————

➤
➤
➤

#2 ——————————

➤
➤
➤

#3 ——————————

➤
➤
➤

#4 ——————————

➤
➤
➤

#5 ——————————

➤
➤
➤

PAGE 24

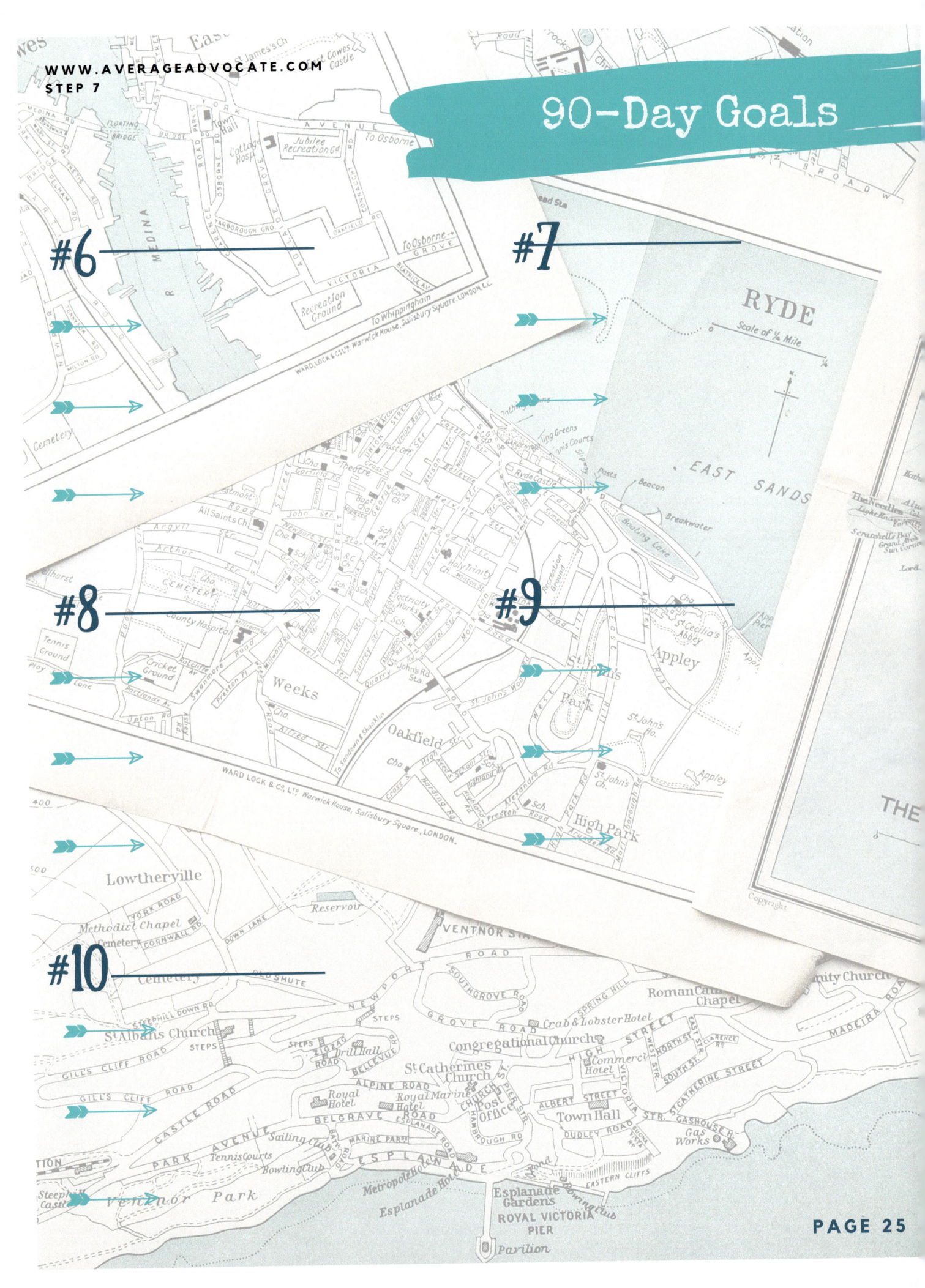

WWW.AVERAGEADVOCATE.COM
STEP 7

90-Day Goals

#6 _____

▶▶ →
▶▶ →
▶▶ →

#7 _____

▶▶ →
▶▶ →
▶▶ →

#8 _____

▶▶ →
▶▶ →
▶▶ →

#9 _____

▶▶ →
▶▶ →
▶▶ →

#10 _____

▶▶ →
▶▶ →
▶▶ →

PAGE 25

STEP 8

Inspiration + Quotes

Your mission in Step Eight is to find at least one quote, scripture, motto, or mantra for each of your Priority Accounts. These should be words that inspire you to imagine your envisioned Ideal Future. The right quotes will strongly motivate you and resonate deeply. These are words to live by; a sail to catch the wind. Write, doodle, or collage them on these pages. You can also add these later as they come to you.

Inspiration + Quotes

Schedule Blocking

I thought Schedule Blocking was a pointless exercise when I first embarked on it. For one, I didn't even like scheduling! To function, I had adapted to using a calendar and even setting aside days or chunks of time for specific purposes. This seemed extra. In addition, Schedule Blocking was a lot of work and I didn't think it would make much of a difference with my time management problems. Boy, was I wrong!

The conceptualization of an "Ideal Week" originally came from Todd Duncan. In order to treat our time as a precious resource that isn't misused, we create a budget for it. We treat it with financial wisdom, designating it to categories so it doesn't get wasted or overspent. Schedule Blocking is our method to budget time.

Intentionally designating your time for each season can be a life-changer.

Of course, we never have 100% control over our time (maybe even 60% is a stretch). But don't get hung-up on that. This works a baseline for your routine.

I call it "Schedule Blocking" because an analogy that works well for my clients is to think of their time like Legos. You are given a limited number of blocks. You can move them around, stack them up, or exchange the red block for the yellow one on any given week. But they all still have to fit. This gives us a level of flexibility once the time budget is established.

"The unexamined life is not worth living."
—Socrates

Schedule Blocking

WWW.AVERAGEADVOCATE.COM
STEP 9

Sunday

Monday

Tuesday

Wednesday

Thursday

Friday

Saturday

Establishing your blocked ideal week schedule can be very hard. It is extremely difficult to be realistic about how much time driving, errands, and random conversations with kids or neighbors actually can take. It is hard to accept what we can't change, which also must get blocked on our baseline schedule. We might have to change up our goals to match our schedule. Another challenge is that it requires us to say "no." However, these challenges can also all be empowering, as ultimately Schedule Blocking helps you become who you are meant to be.

Even though I've been doing this for many years, I still pull out Schedule Blocking when I'm entering a new season or struggling with time management. It is often the first exercise I go to for a new client who doesn't work a 9-5 job or is working on a project they haven't figured out how to make time for.

Schedule Blocking can't solve everything, but it is an excellent tool to begin managing your time. Make a draft on the following page. Then move it to a fresh paper that you can tape up in your kitchen. You can also input it on your phone's calendar to overlay on top of your events calendar. Find examples, spreadsheet templates and other resources for Schedule Blocking with the QR code in the back of this workbook at AverageAdvocate.com.

Schedule Blocking teaches us how to become realistic and recalibrate when we forget what we are supposed to be doing. It empowers us to align with our priorities!

PAGE 29

Schedule Blocking
Guidance as you go

Are you making time for what's important to you? Color code your priorities to ensure each one has time scheduled for them. Ex: green is for community, purple is for work/career.

If it works for you, give your days themes. Ex: Tues. and Thurs. are for meetings; Mondays are for house cleaning.

Be sure to schedule rest and self-care!

Are you realistic about how you spend your time? Ex: if you are carpooling for two hours a day but think it takes "no time at all," use a clock to time it!

Where do you typically lack discipline? Scheduling time helps! Ex: exercising or time for food prep.

Who needs more time invested in them? Ex: playing with kids a few minutes each day, or "pillow talk" with your spouse.

What time for projects needs to be scheduled? Ex: you can write a novel in a month if you have a few hours a day dedicated—but if you only have three hours a week, it might take five years. A more realistic goal is to write an outline or chapter.

What do you forget to make time for? Ex: typing up your meeting notes, or changing baby's diaper, getting his bottle, and buckling him in the car seat.

After making a draft, evaluate where you can realistically "cut-back" on spending your time. Expect that it might take weeks of reevaluation to get your ideal week schedule set up.

When implemented, use it as a guide for scheduling. Ex: 9am-12pm is for work; Wednesdays are for coffee with a friend or random appointments, but 1pm-2pm is for lunch and rest.

When you realize that you're wasting time, refer back to your ideal week to know what to do. If it says rest, don't feel guilty for resting!

Exchanging blocks of time as needed. Ex: if you go on a date on Thurs. instead of Fri., you can't still go out on Fri., but will have to do your Thur. night plans on Fri. instead.

If you can't exchange time blocks, evaluate what will be lost. Is it worth the cost for you? Be smart with your flexibility. Ex: is it worth the cost of dissolving your "cooking dinner" block to spend extra time at the office? Maybe it is.

This tool should serve you; you don't serve it!

Use the following page as a draft, then clarify it in your planner. Use the QR code to find my example and the Google and Excel templates I use.

WWW.AVERAGEADVOCATE.COM   STEP 9   SCHEDULE BLOCKING

MON.	TUES.	WED.	THUR.	FRI.	SAT.	SUN.

NOON

PAGE 31

WWW.AVERAGEADVOCATE.COM
STEP 10

IMPLEMENTATION SYSTEM

Making your Life Map is a great project, but to move towards who you're meant to be it must actually be used! That is why this next step is to create a plan for implementation. Thankfully, you get to create a system that works for you! Design your plan below by checking the boxes:

- ☐ Compile your Life Map into document form to easily view and make new copies of it without doing as much work for future revamps.

- ☐ Print a checklist of your 90-Day Goals and put them by your computer.

- ☐ Put your ideal week block schedule up on your fridge.

- ☐ Hire a designer or use a nice font to display your Purpose Statements in an attractive wall hanging.

- ☐ Because we drift without realigning on a regular basis, choose a time each week to look over your purpose and goals.

- ☐ Do a weekly "brain dump" to clear your head and make a to-do list. Then categorize by priority/project.

- ☐ Choose a "daily three" of smaller goals each day to keep you on track.

- ☐ Break down your goals into smaller tasks and then assign your dedicated project time on your blocked schedule to these tasks.

- ☐ Schedule a few hours every three months to make new goals.

- ☐ Alternatively, have your goals follow the rhythms of the year. Choose new goals for winter/spring, summer, and then the fall. You can also add a more concise set of goals for the holiday season in December, which tends to look very different for many of my clients in the States.

- ☐ Choose a special day once a year to revamp and review your Life Map—What can you celebrate? Are you going the direction you want to be going? How should you adjust?

- ☐ Plan on being gracious to yourself each time you don't meet up to your own standards.

- ☐ Commit to picking up your Life Map when you "fall-off the bandwagon." You'll still have the rest of your life!

- ☐ _____

- ☐ _____

- ☐ _____

Living intentionally is a cycle of review, plan, and execute.

WWW.AVERAGEADVOCATE.COM
STEP 10

IMPLEMENTATION SYSTEM

Map out any other ideas you have below:

When today doesn't go as planned, take a breath. You can start again tomorrow.

Compass & Path

By now you should have a much clearer idea of your destination (*Be*) and how to chart a path to get there (*Do*). I am confident Life Mapping will continue to guide you as you keep moving forward towards an intentional and impactful life.

Before we part ways, I have one more challenge for you! In a couple of sentences, try to summarize your Be and your current dream of Do:

Be:

Do:

What's Next?

WWW.AVERAGEADVOCATE.COM

Congratulations! You finished Life Mapping! This is a valuable achievement worth feeling proud of and grateful for. Tell someone! Post about it on social media! Find a way to celebrate! What an accomplishment! Even if you never do another set of goals, I hope this process has clarified who you are, your direction, and empowered you.

I realize some of you might not feel as confident as you hoped you would at the end of this. If this is you, here are some other signs you might need to consider coaching in addition to filling out this workbook:

- You thrive with accountability
- You still can't find time for this
- You need personal instruction
- You can't muster any vision
- You have too many ideas
- You need encouragement from someone who believes in you
- You can't figure out scheduling
- You don't know what you want
- You keep trying new career paths
- You feel stuck in your movement
- You are overwhelmed by responsibility
- You don't know what makes you tick
- You struggle breaking down your projects

If one or more of these describe you, please reach out. I love coaching people through their Life Mapping process. We will start with a short, free no-pressure discovery call where we can see if we'll be a good fit. In addition to life coaching, I also practice co-active coaching. I have a specialty in helping changemakers (nonprofit leaders, activists, those starting social good initiatives, and ministries) and creatives (writers, podcasters, and other communicators).

Learn more or schedule a discovery call at AverageAdvocate.com/coaching

Thank you for letting me be part of charting your path forward! I am so excited for you as you intentionally pursue who you are meant to be and begin making the difference you're born to make!

Elisa Johnston
YOUR LIFE MAPPING GUIDE

Average Advocate Coaching

WWW.AVERAGEADVOCATE.COM

Resources

As promised, here is a list of extra free tools on my website to equip you on your Life Mapping journey:

- Life Mapping templates
- Life Mapping examples
- Spreadsheet schedule
- Purpose Roadmap
- Values exercise
- Faith Companion for Life Mapping
- References to related resources

Lastly, I wanted to equip you with the names of some of the leaders I've learned from. Their content has shaped this workbook. If you are ready to dive deeper into coaching practices, I recommend starting here! Many have podcasts, Ted talks, YouTube Videos, and Books worth checking out!

Simon Sinek, Stephen Covey, Thomas J. Leonard, Bill Burnett, Dave Evans, Greg McKeown, Denise Massey, Donald Miller, Tony Stoltzfus, Kate Riney, Patrick Williams, Daine S. Meneendez, Chalene Johnson, Michael Hyatt and Daniel Harkavy

AVERAGEADVOCATE.COM/LIFE-MAPPING-RESOURCES

Life Mapping Resources

LIFE MAPPING, PAGE 36

About the Author:

Elisa Johnston is a coach, consultant, podcaster, writer, and speaker. Through her experience founding nonprofits and in activism, she guides everyday changemakers to do good better with more confidence and less overwhelm at AverageAdvocate.com. On Substack @ Authentically Elisa, she also writes about paradigms, changing faith, mental health, and chronic illness for those who are hungry for real talk.

Whenever and wherever she can, she explores with her four kids between the mountains and the sea in her home of San Diego. Thankfully, God, her husband, and other favorite introverts are all particularly grounding. Otherwise, her passion to live missionally, raise up leaders, and start more world-changing things would likely compel her into a creative oblivion.

Average Advocate Coaching

Made in the USA
Columbia, SC
04 July 2025